I0578780

Reckoning: Creativity and Coronavirus
Print Edition: Summer 2021

Reckoning *is a communal effort.*
Editorial staff, in alphabetical order:

Leah Bobet
Cécile Cristofari
Noa Covo
Julia DaSilva
Michael J. DeLuca
Danika Dinsmore
Mohammad Shafiqul Islam
Andrew Kozma
Giselle K. Leeb
Johannes Punkt
Gabriela Santiago
Waverly SM
Catherine Rockwood
Aïcha Martine Thiam
Hal Y. Zhang

Cover and text ornament by Mona Robles

Reckoning Press
206 East Flint Street
Lake Orion, MI 48362
www.reckoning.press
distributed by IngramSpark
printed by Book Mobile
on 100% post-consumer recyled paper.
 ISSN 2474-7327
e-ISBN 978-1-955360-01-2
print ISBN 978-1-955360-02-9

Reckoning:
Creativity and Coronavirus

Contents

A Coronavirus Call for Answers

Michael J. DeLuca

Dear Everyone,

I hope you're safe and healthy and away from risk; I hope you've got somebody to be with in this. I hope you're settling in. Getting comfortable, if you can. It becomes clear this isn't going to be over quick. Everything has been happening so fast, but there's going to be time to think, to process. For some of us, anyway.

I'm as safe as one can be, where I am: as of yesterday Michigan is third in the US for confirmed cases, and Oakland County is second in the state, ever so slightly beating out Detroit. But I'm isolated, in my own house, with a lot of homebrewed beer and homemade preserves in the basement, a sourdough starter in the fridge, woods, meadows and marshes in walking distance. The garden will be popping soon. I'm home schooling my kid, there's only one of him, it's not too bad. I always worked from home.

As for my mental health? I find I want to hear how everyone's doing all the time. I start to feel like a broken record, asking, but at this same moment in which I've never felt less confident in the human capacity to communicate, meaningfully and accurately, I'm also suddenly deeply invested in the everyday boringness of my neighbors, my sisters and my kid's best friend's mom trying to figure out how to teach their kids. I want constant reaffirmation that everyone is as okay as they can be under these extraordinary circumstances.

I know a lot of people aren't.

Environmental justice is a public health issue. This pandemic is exacerbated by climate change, just like extreme weather events, refugee crises and xenophobia. And the people worst hit by it are the people without a safety net: the poor, marginalized, colonized, refugees, people who were already dependent on health care, people who've been drinking and breathing pollution all their lives, people without the option to self-isolate, people who've been given every reason to distrust the voice of authority. To have spent all this time learning to recognize these effects, preparing to watch them get slowly worse, only to suddenly see that change accelerate exponentially and in real time, is devastating, and has only intensified the feeling that I need to do more—the same feeling that made me start Reckoning in the first place.

So I appealed to Reckoning contributors and staff—some of the people I trust and root for most in the world—to let me know how they're doing, and to think together about where this is going. This is the result: Creativity and Coronavirus, a series of short essays and poetry on living, thinking for and creating about the future in this time of crisis.

We might end up doing more, but for now, this is it. New words every Monday, as they're written, until we run out, starting today. Subscribe here, it's free. As always, Reckoning is a publicly funded non-profit; your support is deeply appreciated though not required. We're always open to submissions, actively seeking all kinds of writing from marginalized voices. Please submit.

Be safe.

Michael J. DeLuca is the publisher of *Reckoning*. He's also involved with the indie ebookstore Weightless Books, and his short fiction has been appearing since 2005 in markets such as *Beneath Ceaseless Skies*, *Mythic Delirium* and *Apex*. A novella, *Night Roll*, came out from Stelliform Press in 2020 and was a finalist for the Crawford Award. He lives in the rapidly suburbifying post-industrial woodlands north of Detroit with wife, kid, cats, plants and microbes. Find him on twitter @michaejldeluca.

The Solace of Connection

Marissa Lingen

"Thank God we have the work," my godmother and I keep saying to each other, "thank God we have the work, I don't know what we'd do without the work." She's a painter, and I write. We said it last year when my dad, her big brother, died unexpectedly. We're saying it now.

Everyone copes differently with stress. For me, writing is a solace, but I sometimes get afraid of saying so because people use that as a bludgeon on themselves: if someone else can do it, why can't I? Because people vary. People and circumstances vary. So in addition to the novel I'm still revising, I've written two stories I wouldn't have thought of without this, not about plagues or pandemics or anything like that, but still, two completely new from scratch stories. This happened when my dad was in the hospital, too. Different things came to me. The exhaustion came later.

What kind of world will that exhaustion come into? I honestly don't know. I don't think any of us does. My hope is that we will have an awareness of how connected we all are, whatever happens. There will be terrible losses, both of people and of the kind of small, quirky institution that does some of the best work for change. We are long past the point where we can pretend that those losses won't happen, and to do so would be inhumane. But I do have some faint hope that while we will mourn them individually, we will come away with a clearer understanding of what kind of global ecosystem we really do live in. We can't say, "this is China's problem," or "this is Italy's problem." Like so much else, it is a human problem, it is a global problem.

The very act of trying to isolate shows us how isolated we aren't, we can't be. I hope we'll remember and learn from that. Since we have to be here, we might as well look around, look closely, and try to learn something. I hope it's that no one is truly isolated. I hope it's that none of us, not one of us, is expendable.

—March 28, 2020

Marissa Lingen is a freelance writer living in the suburbs of Minneapolis with her family. Mostly she writes speculative fiction. She has a large collection of foliage-themed jewelry.

Pandemic life.

Casey June Wolf

Pandemic life.

Resting on my bed dayindayout typingmousingtyping frantic to meet these deadlines—Irish immersion, rushing by like the Shannon in flood—tá mé go maith, cad é an t-am é, dé luain dé máirt dé luain dé máirt dé luain dé máirt *dé ceadoin*—and meanwhile this mad massive dive into all things wild boar—where did you come from, fine piggy, fine sow? How did you grow so great? And the spear that took you down, and your bristles that crown the helmets of fine Celtic warriors, and all those piglets swinging from your teats.

Till my neck hardens, head pounds, back screams but—ah!—the luxury of unbroken days to work and eat and feed the birds and stretch these aching bits. No appointments. Few interruptions. *Ahhh.*

But no walks. No visits. Except online, on phone and online; who knew (I knew!) the things that we could do if only we decided. But why did it take catastrophe to bring us here?

Waiting for the words. Who will die?

Here's a surprise. My sister, never one to look these things straight on if she can avoid it, suddenly and silently working out her will, and who will take her daughter, and who will take her sons, if she should fall?

Saddens me. Unthinkable. One father down. The mother must remain.

We are all afraid. But we are stretching in ways we never thought to stretch. My brother with one lung as of days ago, and all of us scattered across the globe reaching him through telephones and chat forums and webcams. Letting him know, baby brother, *we are here.*

One friend tells me *stayathome!* and brings me food. Another puts her scanner outside my door, touches palm to my palm through the glass, picks up the duct tape left there, retreats. One more brings a table and a chair so I can sit outside and be somewhere else but *in-here.*

There is joy in this calculated loving. There is joy in having time to read and think and write what we must write. A language is trickling into me. A beautiful vision of an enigmatic beast and how another species came to see it, reflect it, live on it, deify it, strive to embody it steadily grows with every paper I consume, every tale I review, every voice that speaks to me of the great and bristled boar. It will coalesce, I know it. Chants will come of it. Dreams will come of it. Looking in and seeing who and what we can be and are—all of this will come of it, and soon. Deadlines, recall.

While on my feeder a red-lined cloak flares and folds: the flicker male with his stabbing beak. Finches settle. chickadees quarrel. Sparrows hophophop.

It is a beautiful thing. There is death and life together in this moment as never before. My brother soon to leave us. My sister fearing for her life—with reason, I should say. And me, alone yet not alone, in pain and relative safety, drinking in the sight of juncoes on my step, the sound of small birds muttering, the cool air settling toward night. And the Irish washes in. The boar rouses my blood and makes me seek. And the kindnesses abounding among friends and strangers carries me away.

—March 30, 2020

Casey June Wolf is a poet and writer of occasional, mostly speculative short stories which have appeared in a variety of magazines and anthologies. Recent publications include "Moth Woman on a Dark Night" in *Stellar Evolutions*, and "Eating Our Young" in *Exile Quarterly 43.2*. You may find short essays and links to more of her writing at her blog Another Fine Day in the Scriptorium. Her book *A Brigit of Ireland Devotional: Sun Among Stars* (under the pen name Mael Brigde) is available for pre-order. A collection of speculative fiction, *Finding Creatures & Other Stories*, was published in 2008.

Casey lives in Vancouver, Canada.

COVID Protease Monster Glyph

Mona Robles

I modeled the colors after the contrast depictions by scientists, it spews a black smoke tar because it attacks the lungs, I kept the red accents to underline how dangerous the virus is.

Mona is an indie artist from Mexico who makes monsters inspired in the Classic Maya Period's glyphs, aesthetic and mythology. She digs comics, animation and creature design.

COVID19

Tania Fordwalker

I'm in Tasmania, and here, it's starting to look like we're beating the virus. Every day, the numbers fall. Yesterday, there were zero new infections.

We closed our borders hard and early. We sent people home; we made rules. We're in total lockdown—that's why we're winning.

The streets are so quiet and empty I feel as though I've been transported back to my childhood in the 1980s, to a world only half as crowded as the one we inhabit now. There's no more struggling out of bed on too little sleep to sit in the car among too much traffic on a commute that runs too long. No constant hum of engines outside. No takeout meals. No rushing from work to university to side gigs to home. My schedule filled every second of my life, before. Now I can suddenly breathe again, and it's shocking. We lived in a world that guaranteed—that required—constant growth: more work, more money, more efficiency, more fitness, more possessions, more, more, more. When constant growth occurs in the body, we call it cancer but when it happens in society, in industry, we call that normal.

It's all stopped—paused, anyway. And I feel guilty, because though what's happening to the world is a disaster like nothing in living memory, on a personal level I am free. My creative practice has the space it always needed and never had. My day job has us working from home, giving back all the time I previously lost on commutes. My country has brought in financial safety nets to keep the newly unemployed afloat. Many laid-off casual workers are making more money now than they did before. A surprising number of landlords are easing up on rent and reaching out to their tenants as human beings. The AirBnB owners who sucked all the properties out of the market and left local people fighting for rentals are suddenly, desperately looking for tenants, and we have our choice of homes at reasonable prices for the first time in years. The crushingly overpriced property market is about to crack, giving millenials the long-lost opportunity to own their own homes. We are finally helping the people who need help. The rich have always been able to help themselves.

If we are determined that nobody should have to pay for a cure for COVID-19, why do we accept people paying for cancer treatment? For heart surgery? For insulin? What makes *those* deaths acceptable over *these* deaths? Wouldn't it be better to build a protective society geared towards resilience, so that when things go wrong the ground doesn't collapse underneath us?

I'm not celebrating what's happening. I'm saying we need to examine the sweeping changes we're making, and ask ourselves: was the way we lived before necessary? Was it kind? Was it *working*? If so, why did we have to change it so drastically when the virus came?

The system had already failed so many of us. It just took the horror of COVID-19 to show us how. Defaulting back to 'business as usual' would be a mistake. COVID-19 is the first pandemic of this severity we've seen in living memory, but it may not be the last. We have an opportunity to remake ourselves—to grow stronger, and kinder, and better at taking care of each other.

—April 1, 2020

Tania Fordwalker lives two lives. In one, she's an illustrator and art director for tabletop games. In another, she writes speculative short stories and YA novels. The thread that binds her varied work together is the desire to make people feel something. Working from her home studio in Tasmania's mysterious far south, Tania loves hiking, cider, good movies, bad movies, and building a real corker of a fire in the wood stove. You can find her work online at www.TaniaWalker.com.

Papa's Scary Talk About COVID-19 and Pollution

Tim Fab-Eme

Again, Papa drags the TV remote from my little girl,
his grimace listing all the ills of our nowadays children—
true, such headiness didn't exist even in my own time;
and once they start the territorial dance of Agama agama
I quickly zip my lips and run into the kitchen
before his festering eyes ask how she became a dictator.

Mia's a swashbuckler—I feign cackles and cheer her CBeebies.
I don't know why Papa likes cold wars. Maybe, he
envies her for having all the things he only read
about in his own childhood. But I don't bother him
about the things he couldn't give me in my childhood.

Papa pressed the remote the way Mia traps roaches. CNN.
COVID-19 has hit world trade. Nigeria would learn to drink
her crude oil, to stuff her lungs with greenhouse gases/
It's a beautiful thing, you know, Papa announces. I shriek.

But people are dying, I say. He shakes his head
like a mantis. *There's less pollution now, you know.* Silence.
Good walks with evil—and that's a fact, you know.

I nod and Papa plays on: *Our globetrotting politicians being
home with us is wonderful, you know.* Silence. *Think, son.*

Papa talks the way Mama talked the night she died.

—*April 1, 2020*

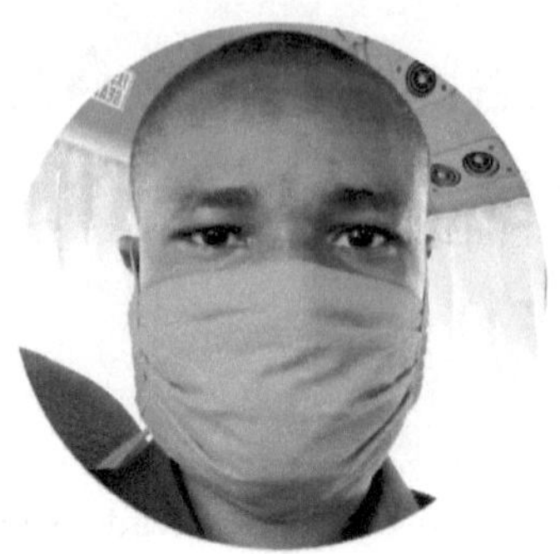

Tim Fab-Eme enjoys playing with poetic forms and the themes of identity, exploitation and the environment; he loves gardening and sometimes thinks himself a farmer. Tim hopes to revisit his long-abandoned prose manuscripts and treat them the way he treats his poetry manuscripts. He lives in Rivers; his work is published in *The Malahat Review*, *New Welsh Review*, *Magma*; *apt*, *The Fiddlehead* and *FIYAH*, etc. Tim studied engineering at the Niger Delta University, and is presently pursuing a BA in English Studies at the University of Port Harcourt.

We Exist Together

Juliana Roth

As the devastation of the pandemic over the coming months pulls into focus, that the deaths from this virus will in a best-case scenario outweigh the total lives lost in the Vietnam War, I am brought into contact with my personal experiences of grief: my father's death, friends with chronic illnesses, romantic relationships ending, and my feelings of insignificance in impacting global catastrophes: systemic violence, discrimination, land theft, factory farming, environmental pollution. How do you exist in a world where pain and loss exist on such incomprehensible scales? How do you create art? Is it selfish to?

As a strong believer in maintaining a morning routine not only as a spiritual practice, but as a way to intentionally move into my day with clarity, this is where I've found my grounding. Wake early, free write and sketch, meditate, bring my dog outside or better yet for a long walk, take my coffee to my desk and write until my alarm goes off, which signals the start of my work day. Knowing there's an alarm set to bring me into awareness of my responsibilities allows my mind to roam freely.

Then I sit and reply to emails from my stream of freelance clients, switching between tasks, checking off to-do lists as I make a smoothie, walk the dog in a proximity of my home that feels safe and not a selfish risk. After working, I move towards possibilities for community within our new, shared reality. I assist with virtual screenings from my local film society's archives. I have a Zoom happy hour with old friends. My sister-in-law sends me dance videos. I exchange yoga sequences and recipes with a friend in Colorado. I attend virtual sessions with my acting coach. I edit a short film. I attend virtual writing groups. I commit to providing myself with evidence that there are endless possibilities to create, that I am enduring. I commit to joy.

Also apparent in my routine is that I am not dealing with illness myself, nor that of anyone in my immediate circle. Though I've lost thousands of dollars in work and will likely lose more, I am able to live temporarily with my family while I regain my financial independence. I have food. I am safe. These are necessary gratitudes.

But safety is only one metric to track. Though I am staying connected, in service, active, laughing—in my own words written over and over when colleagues and friends check in, "I'm doing well," there are moments when I am not. After a recent two-hour trip to the drive-thru pharmacy to refill medication for my grandmother, I found myself pulling over to scream. I stopped the car a block away from my house and hollered, banging my fists against the wheel. It felt like I was only now aware of weeks of fear and anger I'd pressed deep into my body with all of my *doing*, all of the habits keeping me afloat. Humans are resilient, adaptive, and flexible. The challenge of thriving under these conditions has obvious parallels to the climate crisis and any international tragedy. As with the climate crisis, I wonder how much optimistic visioning is warranted, and possible, under such conditions. How much creative imagining is necessary in order not merely to survive but for a solution to emerge? How many hours before our daily alarm do we need to wake in order to keep ourselves moving forward, and who are the ones doing the waking?

Global, shared grief and (for the most part) shared, large-scale community response reveal a great potentiality within us. This experience also reveals the enormity of bureaucratic and political delays that produce such long held-in screams of *why the hell did it take so long to do something?* Because I see myself as an artist, and am fortunate to be connected to and engaged with other artists, such as those at *Reckoning*, who refuse to let our time under any horrid condition result in total silence, I hope for now what I would hope for during any enormous loss: renewal, rebirth. To begin again. To believe in the simultaneity of loss and hope.

—April 1, 2020

Juliana Roth is the creator of the narrative web series, *The University*, which won Best Web/Pilot at the Los Angeles Film Awards and toured nonprofits and college campuses to raise awareness on survivor justice and consent. She is a 2021 Stowe Story Labs Maven Media Fellowship Finalist and is developing several new independent projects for film and tv. Her creative writing appears in the *Los Angeles Review of Books*, *The Breakwater Review*, *Irish Pages*, among others. She serves as a Media Specialist with Rivertown Film Society, teaches creative writing, and is a member Playwright/Actor with WCT Theatre.

The Pandemic Residency

Octavia Cade

Nearly a year and a half ago, I applied for a residency. Massey University, paired with the Square Edge Community Arts Centre, has a writer-in-residence every year. I only applied to practice applying for things. I didn't expect to get it—and I didn't. The 2019 residency was given to another writer . . . but would I be interested in coming in 2020? Yes, I said, I would.

This residency has never been given to a speculative writer before. I think they gave it to me because New Zealand is hosting WorldCon this year, and having a science fiction writer would be thematic.

WorldCon is a virtual convention now. Pandemic put paid to that. It has put paid to a lot of things.

I arrived less than a week before the entirety of New Zealand went into lockdown. Even then, contagion was changing the expectations of residency. My library reading got postponed. So did the workshop. Then the library closed entirely. The welcome event at the university was scaled down, and then cancelled. I have an office, apparently, in the department of English and Media Studies. Somewhere to be creative.

I've never seen it. The university is shut down as well.

Both Square Edge and Massey asked if I wanted to go home. They were very kind; it would be understandable. I chose not to go. I can self-isolate just as easily here as there . . . and there is something very present about a residency that is so very divorced from expectation. We are all of us, up and down the country, forced to live in the moment.

We are also, I think, forced—speculative writers particularly—to examine our expectations, and how they have turned to prejudice. Many of us have engaged with apocalyptic or post-apocalyptic writing at some point. It's a literature of desolation, and mine has been no different. The experience of emergency, however, has shown our narrative bias in a clear light. People are being kinder, mostly. Across the country, they are putting teddies in windows so that kids, out on their lonely daily exercise, can have a bear hunt.

This is not the stuff from which dystopia is made. We're better than we think we are.

As artists, our creations should reflect that.

I'm struck, particularly, by two of my own post-apocalyptic, post-plague stories, written a couple of years apart. The first was published in *Reckoning*. "The Feather Wall" was about a conservationist, stuck on an off-shore island with an endangered species of bird. Alone. Unhappy. The second, which has just received a tentative acceptance from another publisher, tells of community recovery. People coming together, learning to write about—to talk about—the effects of apocalypse in diverse and inclusive ways. It is a far kinder story.

It is, perhaps, also the more realistic, because it is the kinder story.

Pandemic is a terrible thing, it's true. But it is not the only thing, and it does not define us.

—April 2, 2020

Octavia Cade is a New Zealand writer. Her stories have appeared in *Clarkesworld*, *Asimov's*, and *Shimmer*, amongst others. She attended Clarion West 2016 and loves post-apocalyptic stories and science. One of her bucket list goals is to see a live kakapo (at time of writing there were only 148 left, but their numbers are slowly rising).

Summer Song

Mohammad Shafiqul Islam

It's time for agitation against the dark,
for poetry to watch and adore silence–
now it's no time for hug, kiss, or love.
Last summer when we were far away
I planned a rendezvous by a riverbank–
the warm river having a quiet stream
stirring souls–and to bathe together.
One year already passed, but my plan
hasn't seen the light, because nature
had probably hatched its secret plan
before we dreamt to be a twosome.
I also planted a seed of a shady tree
that grows fragrant flowers and fruits,
but the seed has stopped sprouting up.
Miasmic flowers hit our nostrils hard
damaging smell sense, diffusing odor
Everything seems to collapse forever,
the sky betraying with dark stars too.
We live our life—maybe no one does—
turning anaemic, counting days silently.

—*April 3, 2020*

Mohammad Shafiqul Islam is the author of two poetry collections, most recently *Inner State* (Daily Star Books, 2020), and translator of *Humayun Ahmed: Selected Short Stories and Aphorisms of Humayun Azad*. In February 2017, he was a poet-in-residence at the Anuvad Arts Festival, India, and his poetry and translation have appeared in *Journal of Postcolonial Writing*, *Poem: International English Language Quarterly*, *Critical Survey*, *Stag Hill Literary Journal*, *SNReview*, *Reckoning*, *Dibur Literary Journal*, *Lunch Ticket*, *Bengal Lights*, *Armarolla*, and elsewhere. His work has been anthologized in a number of books, including *The Book of Dhaka: A City in Short Fiction* (Comma Press, UK). Currently at work on a few translation projects such as *The Letters of Kazi Nazrul Islam*, Dr Islam is Associate Professor of English at Shahjalal University of Science and Technology, Sylhet, Bangladesh.

On And About

Innocent Ilo

The messages are urgent—create more art now, document your experiences in these times, don't sweat over if what you're creating makes sense, the world needs it, you need it. I create art, mostly short fiction, and I have to do it while battling with depression and anxiety. No, I cannot write through my depressive and anxiety episodes. I wait patiently for those rare moments of mental clarity to create art. These moments of mental clarity have become even rarer during this pandemic with my Twitter feed choked with news about yet another confirmed case of the Covid-19 virus or how testing is still inaccessible for most people or how health workers are on the frontline with limited personal protective equipments. So any attempt to write funnels into hours of staring at a blank word document until I exit the window with a What am I doing? Does the world really need this?

Away from my crushing anxiety, the world outside my window is in sharp contrast with the one inside my head. It is bubbly and almost detached from the present. This is the world I've grown to find solace in during these times. As part of the strategy to contain the virus, the Lagos State Government shut down schools. So, the schoolchildren in the block of apartment I live in have devised a means to keep themselves busy. Just before noon, they gather in the quadrangle and take turns teaching themselves literature, mathematics, and science. There are breaks in between and assignments. Their laughter and arguments over who got the multiplication problem wrong wake me from my afternoon nap. In the evenings, the once-busy street is filled with kids playing football. Neighbors who could go weeks without seeing each other because of their busy jobs sit in front of shops drinking beer and eating street food. It is an infectious atmosphere (no pun intended). There is a growing sense of community and a growing interest in other people's well-being. This is something people normally do not have time for in this rise-hustle-and-grind city.

Not creating fiction of my own has also given me more time to do what I love; discovering and rediscovering the beauty of other people's works through reading. I have tripled my reading, from published works to solicited drafts from friends. There is a comfort that comes with the assurance that someone else is writing and documenting about/through this epoch when you can't. I am also thinking about if and how this period will leave a mark on my craft? How lasting will this mark be? Will it be me doing too much? Will it be me doing too little? And when these questions begin to overwhelm me, I look at the world outside my window and find the calmness I seek.

—*April 5, 2020*

In between receiving tonnes of rejections from cat adoption agencies, Innocent finds time to read, write, tweet and nurse his fragile ego. His works have been published or are forthcoming in *Fireside*, *Strange Horizons*, *Brittle Paper*, *SSDA* and elsewhere.

A Predicament

Johannes Punkt

Editor's note: In the submission call for this series, I asked everybody to answer two questions: how has the pandemic affected your creative practice, and how will the world change?

The short answer, Michael, is that I will change nothing and I doubt the world will change. The slightly longer answer is that the world has always been unravelling: in our lifetimes, there have been multiple genocides and there hasn't been a single day without apartheid or war. As I'm fond of saying, the apocalypse is already here—it's just not very evenly distributed.

A predicament many writers are suddenly facing, staring into the white eye of pandemic, is this: how can we write something that feels true if what's true keeps being beaten, burnt up, disappeared, diseased, disintegrated, dissolved, eviscerated—gutted like a fish, pulled away from under us, quarantined, quashed, revealed to have been lies and slander? How can we write something real? How can we put pen to paper to lovingly describe the deck chairs on the Titanic when the ship is sinking and *they won't keep still*?

First, reader, if this is the first time you're feeling this particular feeling of the world being sucked into the drain, vorticing your words away and mixing your metaphors with sewage water and rising bile, and I say this without meaning to be flippant or to dismiss the very real panic, congratulations. Up until now you, somehow, had comparative stability. You were, somehow, not living with the threat of climate change that keeps thrumming the threads of all our lives vibrating right next to your ear. Or a myriad of the other things that threaten to devour us. You were making sandcastles at the top of the hourglass. You may have known about the threat of literal apocalypse, but you didn't feel it bodily. That's good, for your life. That's good.

At some point in the history of literature, the horizon crashed into the International Date Line and all fiction that was being written turned into speculative fiction. I don't know exactly when that was, because the International Date Line is imaginary, but maybe it was the day after the Berlin Wall was razed. Maybe it was the day before Iceland fined and imprisoned its bankers that had caused the economy to collapse. Maybe it was yesterday, but I doubt it. More to the point, there is no longer such a thing as fiction that is not speculative.

Normally, in the world you thought you lived in before, speculative fiction was the catch-all term for a specific market of fiction dominated by science fiction and fantasy, but where other genres such as steampunk, horror, alternate history, and the like also resided. In this definition, writing with strong similarities to speculative fiction but which comes from a tradition of more *literary or mainstream* elements, such as slipstream, magical realism, modern fairy tales and technothrillers, has usually not been included under the umbrella. This division is purely market-based, as all genres are. What defines speculative fiction is a point of departure from our world: a man with giant batwings under his suit, telekinesis, a portal through a mirror to another world, the continents on Earth itself being arranged differently, the year 3001, Napoleon victorious at Waterloo. The points of departure are different in nature, but they are all flipped variables. 0 to 1. In our world, the one you used to live in, the Soviet Union did *not* put a man on the Moon before America did. In the world you used to inhabit, freak storms did not sink all of Columbus' fleet. In that world, Neanderthals didn't evolve parallel to us. But what if they did? And so on.

Some variables are more influential than others; some changes cascade other changes. What you're experiencing is whole arrays turned into garbage code, though, and it's natural to not be able to parse this. Some of you have felt this before, and maybe the only thing that made you able to create art again was manually going down to the fuse box of your life and flipping the variables one by one: *not homeless anymore, not in love with that asshole, five thousand kilometres away from family, eleven days without skipping a meal, twelve days without skipping a meal, thirteen days without skipping a meal.*

You're not going to have that much access to that fuse box while the societal web is tearing. But the principle remains the same.

This is not a controversial statement: all fiction is based on points of departure from the world you believed yourself to be a part of, because otherwise it wouldn't be fiction. So the thing that separated speculative fiction from the other fiction, disregarding the market argument, was the nature of the variable. The point of departure was such that the world felt like a different place, right? And now, when you think back on a working class novel from the 1980s that you've read, it uncannily feels like it was written in a different world. But it hasn't changed. It is merely speculative, and you're seeing it.

So, you don't know which variables do what in the web you're seeing unravelling. You're standing in your indoor sandals in the basement, flipping light switches and trying to get the floor to stop yawning open. If you're a speculative writer already, you might have an advantage here, because you already know how to scout for the variables. If there's no ink when you try to type, you probably need to imagine the world you're writing in first. You don't have to write what you know, you can take one variable at a time. (It's always like that in trying to make the world better than it is, which is what you should be trying to do.) Speculate. Rinse, repeat. Depart.

April 5, 2020

Johannes Punkt is a writer, translator and alarmist from Sweden whose texts occasionally surface. He's been part of the Reckoning Editorial Staff since the second issue. Email: johannes@reckoning.press. (Photograph courtesy of Josefin Tollgren.)

A Memory of the Future

Floris M. Kleijne

"Mom? Why does this freeway have so many lanes?"

"Well Tom, remember when you were six, and the schools were all closed, and you did all your schoolwork as homework? And your teacher came on Zoom every day?"

"Er . . . yes?"

"Well . . . remember, before that time, that your Dad and I went away to work at the office every weekday?"

"What? No. Why would you?"

"Good question, Tom. Why did we? Why did everyone?"

"Dunno. Makes no sense to me. I mean, you only go to the office when you have to be there, right? Otherwise, what's the point of the whole communism?"

"Commute."

"Yeah, yeah, the commute. What's the point of commuting if you can do . . . whatever it is you do, from home?"

"Thing is, people used to think that was necessary to come to the office every day before nine, and work from there, and hold meetings with everyone in the same room. People were convinced—your dad and I were convinced as well, that all of us gathered together in the same building was the only way to have a productive workday."

"But . . . that's weird. Didn't you have internet? Couldn't you Zoom? Or Teams, or whatever?"

"Oh no, we did have internet, and Teams, and everything. But we only used those for people who couldn't come in to the office."

"So everyone else would drive to the office *every day*? That's . . . like . . . thousands of people, isn't it?"

"Yep."

"Wouldn't they fill up all these lanes, then?"

"Yep . . . more than fill."

"What do you mean?"

"There would be so many cars every morning that they'd

all get stuck. And this traffic congestion would mean they'd all be crawling along. This whole stretch of freeway, from where we got on, to the exit for my office, takes about twenty minutes by car. But mornings, your dad and I both spent at least an hour in our cars here."

"You're kidding, right?"

"Not kidding. And all those cars would belch out exhaust fumes."

Tom mulled this over for a while.

"Boy, I'm glad everyone came to their senses," he said. "Do you want some water?"

He stopped walking and shrugged out of his backpack. Pulling the water bottle from the side netting, he handed it to Mom. Just ahead, road workers were tearing out the tarmac of the fourth and fifth lanes. Further down the freeway, they could see where the two lanes had already been turned into a strip of greenery, a bike path and a walking trail.

On the three remaining lanes, a steady stream of cars made their way to the commercial district on the horizon. Tom tried and failed to imagine all five lanes jammed with cars. He shrugged and looked to the side. In the distance, the North Sea sand dunes shimmered in the growing summer heat. Mom grabbed his arm.

"Look!"

She was pointing at the nearest field, where a doe was calmly grazing.

"Me too," she said. "I'm glad too."

—April 11, 2020

Floris M. Kleijne writes stories, some of them award-winning, in the interstices between his family, his career in finance, and his insatiable craving for Netflix binges. His stories have appeared in the Writers of the Future anthologies, on *Daily Science Fiction*, in *Spark: A Creative Anthology*, in *Galaxy's Edge* and numerous other publications. He lives in a centuries old farm house in the Dutch river district, with a wonderful wife, two cheerful sons, ten crates of Legos, and thousands of books. Find more of his writing on https://www.floriskleijne.com.

Writing in the Time of Coronavirus

Giselle Leeb

Last night, I dreamt that a campsite I stayed at during a cycle tour was barren, as if there had been a terrible drought. I touched the wall of a house and rubble cascaded down. Then I was walking up a narrow staircase with a man who was escorting me to a job interview with his boss. The staircase wound up and up, getting tighter, until I couldn't go any further.

A few weeks ago, saturated with anxiety, I could hardly concentrate, and repeatedly broke my rule of not looking at the Internet while writing, to obsessively read the news. After a while, I banned myself from reading news in the mornings until I'd done some writing.

At first, I did feel that writing was unimportant, in view of what's going on. Then I thought: you were always going to die and so if writing is meaningless now, it always was. Or wasn't.

Writing is for me a comfort and an affirmation of living, like playing sport or painting or making music, or doing just about anything you enjoy. You've got to love it to do it. Or, you do it because you love it. That doesn't change.

I've just finished the final edits for my short story collection and I've written a number of stories about ecological collapse. I'm now starting work on a cli-fi novel, which inevitably involves some form of apocalypse, whether slow or sudden.

All of my recent writing has ended up being about what's happening to us now. The only difference to my previous writing is that I now have the additional immediate perspective of how I feel—I am, like everybody, directly involved. I'll have to wait and see if this changes how I write.

Writing and being published creates a connection, a communication, with the reader, a telling of your story and everyone's stories. Stories are about understanding life: about suffering, struggle and new possibilities, and simply about what it's like to be alive.

In recent weeks, my love for and anger at my fellow humans

has grown. Anger as people break social-distancing rules. Rage at the government response. And love for people as I read their particular stories of suffering, or losing somebody they love, or the unfairness of unequal exposure to risk caused by economic inequality.

But also, I've had a new feeling that judgements won't work. I don't mean not holding power to account, but rather not blaming people on an individual level for not doing everything they can. Ranting at each other seems less important than trying to listen to each other and think about what really matters. It means changing our doomed consumerist cry from: I deserve it, to: what can I do to fight for everybody?

Good writing is always complicated. Already we are listening more than usual to other people's stories. I just hope there'll always be ways to keep writing and people who will want to keep reading.

—April 12, 2020

Giselle Leeb grew up in South Africa and lives in Nottingham. Her short stories have appeared in over thirty publications including *Best British Short Stories 2017* (Salt), *Lady Churchill's Rosebud Wristlet*, *Black Static*, *Mslexia*, *Litro*, and other places. She is a Word Factory Apprentice Award winner and an assistant editor at *Reckoning Journal*. Her story, Scaffolding, is forthcoming in *Mainstream*, an anthology of stories from the edges, by Inkandescent Press.
http://giselleleeb.com
Twitter: @gisellekleeb

Protecting Edges

Anna Kate Blair

I've been thinking about saltspray roses, rugged and adaptable, clinging to dunes, strengthening coastlines, hardier than their blossoms suggest. I've had trouble writing, lately, because I don't want to expose myself, don't want to publish anything that I might regret, and yet (for me) writing demands vulnerability. I turn my flaws to the light, hoping that I might be human, and so I'm always risking regret when I write. It's impossible to stay safe. I risk it, though, because writing carries possibilities of alchemy and growth, of salted flowers in unexpected places. I see writing as an ecotone, a liminal space in which it feels possible for anything to change, all violence and fertility, elemental and charged with flux.

My favourite outcome of alchemy is intimacy. I am motivated by the conversations, the relationships, that build through writing. In isolation, though, connection is intangible, and there's strength in staying quiet, protecting oneself. I was, when I was younger, guarded and resilient, like a sea wall, made of stone, but I'm trying, now, to be sustainable, integrated, like a saltspray rose, gathering strength through entwining roots with others, leaning into the wind. It takes work to stay tender.

I've found other creative activities, though, that soothe me. I've been learning about tarot cards, shuffling them so often that my thumb has a small blister. I sleep with a sachet of lavender, wake up clutching amethyst, and write down my dreams. I blow on the stems of my indoor plants so as to simulate the air outside, dye my hair with honey and beetroot. I've remembered, like many, that I'm good at cooking. These practices emphasise process and intuition, rather than a finished product, and this feels healthy.

I don't know, when I list these things, if I'm romanticising domesticity. I am lucky to have the time and space for such activities. It feels heartless to witness personal growth against this backdrop of devastation, but it's disingenuous, when asked about creativity, not to acknowledge it. I won't credit it to coronavirus. I was, right before the pandemic's scope became apparent, finally learning to accept loss and uncertain futures, changing in ways that surprised me. I can't separate my response to this pandemic from everything that preceded it.

I'm still trying to write on the edge of my own knowledge, to stop sand from slipping into water. I don't want to soften things with simile, with saltspray roses, and yet we need beauty, or we will. We're at the beginning, still, and I'm expecting grief, anticipating so much loss that mourning is subsumed, death left unprocessed because it's quotidian, everywhere, affecting everyone. I don't feel good. I could write of how the world might change, but trying to smooth the passage into the future can destroy our capacity to cope with the present. I'm struggling to write, but that's fine—growth is difficult, but saltspray roses manage it, in their wild ecotone, and all I need to do is stay inside.

—April 13, 2020

Anna Kate Blair is a writer and architectural historian from New Zealand. She has had work in publications including *Litro*, *The Appendix*, *King's Review*, *Antithesis Journal* and *10 Stories: Writing About Architecture.*

#SayNiceThingsAboutDetroit

Mansuda Arora

There's a certain look people get on their faces when I answer the question of where I'm from. I go to great lengths to assure them I'm not the survivor of apocalypse they expect me to be. Since the beginning of the COVID-19 pandemic, more and more cities will start having to reckon with the torn social safety nets that failed to catch the people of Detroit.

I recently stumbled across the hashtag: #SayNiceThingsAboutDetroit. "We're practically begging at this point," I thought. A few years ago, the city announced they were closing seventy-two parks. The playgrounds and parks where I took my first steps are now paved over or overtaken by wild grasses. The people I loved with their beautiful copper and blue faces have since fled like refugees from their own homes. There are houses on the edge of the city that the land has reclaimed, vines and branches shattering windows, weeds, and cattails overgrowing the lawns. This is where the people who stayed began what the locals call "urban farming" when all the national grocery store chains left. This is subsistence farming. Survival farming. Only once we have our own land can we be free. The land may not be valuable, but the people of Detroit are free.

When I imagine moving back home, I'm afraid the city I knew will have been wiped away completely by the time I return. Before the pandemic, I dreamt that the house I grew up in was overtaken by vines, spilling from windows and shattering the glass. They grew, gripping the indentations between the bricks and down onto the street, filling the cracks in the sidewalks. The buildings began to topple under their weight, first crumbling, then sinking into the earth. In the back of my mind I thanked God that no one was inside, and with that thought, I looked around to find that there was nothing but silence and everyone was gone. No one skating in the park, no one buying hot dogs from the usual vendors, no one loitering on the steps of the library. Not even the police were parked in their usual spot at the intersection corner.

What happens when a city goes bankrupt? City services are

cut down. Fewer trash cans, fewer cops, fewer schools and no one to put out the fires when people would rather burn down their homes and collect the insurance money than make another payment on a home that is falling apart above their heads. The government has given up on our recovery.

The Detroit of the future will be made up of the people who stuck it out, who defended their homes amid disaster. The people of Detroit are survivors of the failed experiment of the American dream, and they are the most beautiful people I have ever known. I know that someday after the world has its reckoning, I will return, and it will not be long before people have something nice to say about Detroit.

—April 14, 2020

Mansuda Zeba Arora is an editorial assistant at Liveright, an imprint of W.W. Norton & Company. She recently received a master's degree in critical media and cultural studies from SOAS, University of London, and has a bachelor's degree from Sarah Lawrence College, where she studied nonfiction writing and sociology. Mansuda is a Gemini, a horror movie fanatic, and a child of the Midwest. She tells true stories.

One Month

E. M. Wright

1,000,000. Number of Covid-19 deaths in the U.S. predicted in a statistical model published March 13th that assumed no social distancing measures.

154. Number of minutes on March 15th that I spent reading news media on my iPhone.

0. Number of states with "stay at home" orders on March 16th.

On March 17th I woke up at 2 a.m. I checked our bank account balances and mortgage. I estimated our average monthly budget. I calculated a budget for us without my husband's income. I calculated a budget for us without my income. I filled a notepad with numbers.

349,000,000,000. Number of dollars the US government allocated on March 27th to a Forgivable Loan Program for small businesses.

100,000. Number of Covid-19 deaths in the U.S. predicted by U.S. officials on March 31st as a "best case scenario."

6. Distance measured in feet to maintain between yourself and any non-household member.

On March 29th I woke up at 4 a.m. I read The New York Times. The Guardian. FiveThirtyEight. *My local newspaper.* The Washington Post. Vox. *I needed more. More facts. More graphs and charts. More ways to control the uncontrollable.*

6,650,000. Number of Americans who filed a new claim for unemployment benefits during the fourth week of March.

5. Number of times I used hand sanitizer during a trip to the grocery store on April 3rd.

55. Number of diagnosed Covid-19 cases in my county as of April 3rd.

On April 4th I woke up at 2 a.m. to read the news. I read for hours. And hours.

6. Number of minutes within a timekeeping increment for my law firm.

70. Number of professional increments I need each day within a schedule that has become po-rous, overlapping math tutorials and skinned knees with PowerPoint slides and client consulta-tions.

13. Number of increments I spent on April 7th attending to my professional obligations.

17. Number of increments I spent on April 7th walking through the woods with my children.

During the night of April 8th I slept 9 hours and 40 minutes. I woke tired and slow. After breakfast I put the milk in the pantry instead of the fridge. I stared at my computer screen.

12,621. Number of deaths in the US attributed to Coronavirus as of April 8th.

21,919. Number of deaths in the US attributed to Coronavirus as of April 13th.

28,280. Number of deaths in the US attributed to Coronavirus as of April 16th.

I dream of a corps of poets, deployed to every news conference, stepping forward to the microphones. Come to save us from a world turned inside out. Giving us words to crawl beneath the facts. Words to hold our souls. Words to take root in the places where our stories live. Because those who habitually see the world inside out may be the only ones who can restore our equilibrium in the present moment.

E. M. Wright's work has appeared or is forthcoming in *Berkeley Fiction Review*, *The South Carolina Review*, *Pithead Chapel*, and elsewhere. She holds an MFA from Vermont College of Fine Arts.

Coronavirus and the Digital Divide

Commando Jugendstil

Going into the gradual UK lockdown, two weeks ago, we expected to feel scared, worried for our relatives scattered across the world, and, after a few days of forced inactivity, bored out of our wits. We knew that there was not a lot we could do about the first two, but thankfully our core members had the luck and privilege to be well stocked of craft supplies, books and videogames. However we hardly had a chance to touch any of that.

In fact, most of us in the core team have the privilege to be able to work from home for most of our regular work activities and we have found that without a clear break between work and reproductive labour, the two blend in seamlessly in a continuum of tasks to complete, leaving hardly any interstice to sneak in an hour or so of creativity. This has been the source of a large amount of frustration among our members and we still haven't found a way to build a new work-life balance. Perhaps time will tell, but we're open to suggestions.

Like for most people, our social life has moved to the web. We've been using various video calls to contact family, meet with colleagues and organise with fellow activists and solarpunk creators. Physical distances have been simultaneously made impassable and immaterial. If all places are equally impossible or impractical to reach, there is no reason why collaborating with someone across the ocean would be any harder than doing the same with someone only a few miles away. Endless possibilities are open before us who have a good connection to the web: we can give seminars to faraway universities and collectives, attend lectures from esteemed colleagues five time zones away, reconnect with relatives we've not seen in a decade.

This is all well and good, however this crisis has highlighted how much of a privilege this is. For the people caught on the other side of the digital divide, the shift of all social life, education and services to the web is inevitably another source of stress as it becomes completely inaccessible to them.

When politicians and activists call for net neutrality or even for free internet connection for everyone, they are not trying to "pander to the millennial demographic", but recognising that the internet has become an extension of the public sphere and an essential tool for daily life, and as such it should be treated like a common good with no access barriers.

Between this and the huge surveillance and data ownership issues raised by the recent controversies regarding most social platforms, there has never been a better moment to discuss and design a better way of building and managing the internet, one that centres people's digital rights and privacy instead or profits and is built around democratic self-organisation, free open-source software and cooperativism.

Our hope for the future is that we will collectively learn from this stressful, exceptional experience and build a new, better digital normality.

—April 24, 2020

Commando Jugendstil is a small collective of Italian solarpunk creators who aim to conjugate green technology and art to make cities a better place to live in and build creative communities. So far they have written short stories for *Mamut Magazine no. 6 (Eco-logos)*, the independent UK publisher Bear With Me Books, and the anthologies *Glass and Gardens: Solarpunk Summers* and *Glass and Gardens: Solarpunk Winters* by WorldWeaver Press, and designed artwork for *Mamut Magazine no. 6 (Eco-logos)*, *Optopia Zine vol. 1* and *Ecología Política no. 57 (Las artes y la ecología política)*, among other things. Their members are invested in climate justice activism and are part of Earth Strike UK. They have recently won an EU grant to use solarpunk speculative design to help communities plan and enact their sustainable futures—if all goes well, then a solarpunk reality may not be too far away.

Art Installation in the Time of COVID-19

Krista Hoeppner Leahy

Collaborators:

Wind, sunshine, water,
clouds, fruit, rocks

Text:

my son asks if I have an idea
of what happens when we die

I tell him I don't know but yes
I've ideas, words, approximations

of concepts outsized by my
grasp—eternal, ephemeral,

what is essential work
in these days when luck

unluck has gone viral
and we cannot hold

hands to pluck hope, ripe
fruit needs to be washed

with sunshine, love, will
to create, postponing

questions past our certainty—
who are the gardeners,

what is the garden, I

ask him, what is essential

for creation, for life
growing, blooming, seeding,

he smiles. The wind uplifts
and we are cirrus high

where we marvel at how
much we see and don't know,

hear and cannot understand,
hope and do not know how to

hold.

Music:

rocksplash of rapids,
your unswerving heart

—May 17, 2020

Krista Hoeppner Leahy is a poet, writer, and actor. Her work has appeared in *Clarkesworld, Farrago's Wainscot, Lady Churchill's Rosebud Wristlet, Raritan, Shimmer, Tin House, Year's Best Science Fiction and Fantasy* and elsewhere. With deep thanks to Vermont Studio Center and Banff Centre for Arts and Creativity, for the time and space to write. Born in Colorado, Krista currently resides in Brooklyn with her family.

Looking Out, Looking In

Shikhandin

These days, I am unable to hold on to my days. They are like runaway horses. And the reins are no longer in my control. Strange now, when my life is even more cloistered. I withdrew from the rambunctious world outside when my children grew old enough to be independent. So I could write.

These days I rarely leave my 18th floor apartment. Not even to walk on the lawns and parks of our gated community, a microcosm, self-sufficient and barricaded against the rough and tumble of the world outside. Covid 19 may be my official reason. But I know better. I don't belong. I can't relate to problems arising from dealing with housework and office, because of the absence of an entourage of help—cook, nanny, char-woman or maid, chauffeur and elderly care help for those who have senior citizens living with them. The hysteria that arises because their expensive cars—BMWs, Audis, Mercedes, Jaguars etc. etc.—need to run or else the batteries will die. And the excitement of queuing up, re-usable shopping bags and masks in place, for the various food trucks selling mangoes and other fruits, chicken and mutton and even varieties of Indian desserts. Because well-off Indians need their shopping fix, and if it is only food for sale, well then so be it.

I am a crow living among birds of paradise.

The world has stopped travelling. But Indians have not. They are travelling hundreds of miles, by the hundreds. These are the migrant workers, those nameless, faceless, union-less men and women and sometimes even children, who work for long hours for disgraceful remuneration, and who are now bereft of even that meagre earning.

This is the other face of India. A face that has wiped out my self-centered sorrows at losing my quiet days of uninterrupted routine, because my spouse is working from home, and he naturally gets priority—that is how we were raised, to put ourselves last, and I am a feminist only in theory. That is not the entire truth, though. I have also stopped writing because it suddenly seems like a frivolous activity. But I can't stop writing in my head. As I cook and clean and repeat the chores again and again, the writing continues and disappears, because the words are never 'put down.' I have to look at my cell phone to determine my days. I cannot tell a Sunday from a Monday any more.

Be thankful, be thankful, we tell each other, and our children when we video chat with them.

Sixteen workers were cut up like butcher's meat beneath the wheels of a goods train during the early hours of the night of the flower moon. They were walking home from one end of India to another, thinking they were taking a straight and safe path, because trains were not running during the lockdown. They didn't know about goods trains. Another day, a young man, traveling on the roof of a bus, after shelling out what would have been a fortune for him, collapsed and died in his friend's arms. The day temperatures often rise to 42 degrees Celsius and more. He was not Covid positive. He died of dehydration. There are so many tragic stories being played out. The media catches the dramatic ones and housebound ghouls lap them up.

What should I be thankful for? For myself and my family? We wrap ourselves up in the comfort of our self-centeredness. Life is less complicated. Or would have been if my mind was differently configured.

Looking down from my balcony, at the street dogs chasing each other and the occasional car, the delivery trucks and Swiggy bikes, I watch workers without any kind of protective gear laying underground cables and repairing roads. Across the road, and beyond the boundaries of a posh villa community opposite our own, cranes turn slowly over a high-rise complex, gradually adding to its height.

The ministers say they are helping the economy and also providing jobs for the migrant workers, encouraging them to stay back in the cities. The government has announced financial aid and safe transport for the migrants who are returning home, because they feel it is better to die there among their families than in the cities. The exodus continues. Aided or unaided. Even as the government prepares to lift lockdown and 'normal life' begins to trickle back.

There are other tragedies happening, non Covid ones. These are putting their weight against Covid's devastation. Cyclone Amphan flattened homes and livelihoods in my home state, Bengal.

Swarms of locusts have eaten acres and acres of standing crops in Rajasthan and neighboring states. And they are still feasting as I write.

The gloom and doom are lighter in places though. Good Samaritans, ordinary citizens, and even news reporters interviewing the migrants are stepping in to give what help they can. Even if it means only slippers for their feet and bottles of water. These people are not necessarily the rich. Many are financially needy themselves. Then there are our pharmaceutical companies who are going all out to produce vaccines and medicines. I didn't know before this pandemic that India produces around 70% of the world's vaccines.

My heart remains restless. Suddenly writing to be published seems a frivolous desire. Mending a hole in a T-shirt seems a superior activity. Nevertheless, a week or so ago, I made a conscious effort to sit down at my computer and write, random paragraphs. Those exercises have helped. I am somewhat relieved, because I had written nothing the whole of April.

Sometimes the writing is automatic. As if a creature from my innermost depths has risen to express herself. And it is possibly she who has put this thought to me: what does it matter if nobody ever reads me? If my fiction, poetry, essays etc. never get to see the light of day? How does my writing change anything in the world, anyway? There are thousands of unread books. If I were to choose between one and the other, what would I rather be, the reader or the writer?

My reading life has returned, quietly but firmly. As a child, adolescent, and then as a single adult I used to devour books every day. I felt insecure if I didn't have a book in my bag, even when I went grocery shopping for my mom. Juggling office and children changed all of that. I read to my children when they were small, but had stopped reading for myself. My spouse isn't an avid book reader; he would choose television over a book. None of our acquaintances, personal friends and relatives are. None of them write either, but they have strong opinions about books and writers and the artistic world in general. For many years my reading had been reduced to a trickle, as I tried to straddle my inner and my exterior worlds. A handful of books in a year, instead of the three or four I used to consume in a week. For the past few weeks, I have not sat with my spouse to watch a movie or even the news. I've been reading in between my chores and before going to bed.

I feel I have begun a new journey, albeit a private one. I will not stop writing. But I am now conscious that it is the act of writing that brings me happiness, not seeing it in print. Material success or the lack of it is, well, immaterial. This does not mean I won't send out work anymore. I will, but there is neither hurry nor anxiety now.

The world has changed. I see it as molting into something new, and perhaps terrifying, but definitely different. We don't know who will survive and who won't, who will be able to adapt and who won't. As for me, my place in the world may be less than a dust-mote, but let it be a happy mote of dust. Because that is humanity's triumph against strangeness, against adversity, against calamity. Because humanity knows how to rise again and again. And I am part of it, tiny, insignificant, but a part nevertheless. Stay blessed.

—May 27, 2020

Shikhandin is the pen name of an Indian writer. Her published books include "Impetuous Women" (Penguin-Random House India), "Immoderate Men" (Speaking Tiger), and "Vibhuti Cat" (Duckbill-Penguin-Random House India). Prior to that a novel and a short story collection were published. Shikhandin's honours include, runner up George Floyd Short Story Contest 2020 (UK), Pushcart nominee by Aeolian Harp (USA) 2019, Pushcart nominee by Cha: An Asian Literary Journal (Hong Kong) 2011, Winner 2017 Children First Contest curated by Duckbill in association with Parag an initiative of Tata Trust, First prize Brilliant Flash Fiction Contest 2019 (USA), Runner up Erbacce Poetry Prize (UK), Winner 35th Moon Prize (Writing in a Woman's Voice: USA), First Runner up The DNA-OoP Short Story Contest 2016 (India), Second Prize India Currents Katha Short Story Contest 2016 (USA), First prize Anam Cara Short Fiction Competition 2012 (Ireland), Long list Bridport Poetry Prize 2006 (UK), Finalist Aesthetica Poetry Contest 2010 (UK). Shikhandin's poetry and prose have been widely published in journals and anthologies worldwide.

Amazon Page: https://www.amazon.com/author/shikhandin
Facebook: https://www.facebook.com/AuthorShikhandin/
Instagram: https://www.instagram.com/writershikhandin/
Twitter: @Shikhandintweet

Dynamic Equilibrium

Teika Marija Smits

Looking at a fluid-filled conical flask,
the reactants colourless,
you'd think nothing of note was happening.

It's been the same of life in lockdown:
we go nowhere, see no one, touch nothing.

And yet, my son has taken up jogging and cooking,
my daughter, YouTube yoga, art.
My lecturer husband has been finding new ways
to connect with his students.

Me, I've been filling my own flask with words,
pouring myself into stories that one day I'll share.

We've all been planting seeds and learning of the gifts
of nature; this unhurried way of life,
the dynamic quality of patience.

There is nothing static about this;
the very molecules of our being
are rearranging themselves.

—May 31, 2020

Teika Marija Smits is a UK-based freelance editor, writer and mother-of-two. She writes poetry, fiction and non-fiction, and her speculative fiction has been published in *Reckoning*, *Shoreline of Infinity*, *Best of British Science Fiction 2018* and *Enchanted Conversation.* Her debut poetry pamphlet, *Russian Doll*, was published by Indigo Dreams Publishing in March 2021. She is an Editor-at-Large at Valley Press, and in spare moments she likes to draw, paint and doodle. She is delighted by the fact that Teika means fairy tale in Latvian. She can be found online at: https://teikamarijasmits.com and on Twitter as @MarijaSmits

Living in a Metaphor

Waverly SM

I worked on my manuscript, yesterday, for the first time in weeks. I feel creatively, existentially frail; it is hard to think through in the same way I have always assumed that fish find the ocean hard to think through. Immersed in the conditions of your own existence, it's hard to find perspective. The challenge is to learn to see better.

My country, ostensibly a global power, has the highest death rate in Europe. Our leaders never quite *invited* the public to join in street parties on VE Day, but they sure did switch up their messaging on the subject just in time for Little Englanders everywhere to mass in the streets, in misguided celebration of our glorious, defanged history. Blitz spirit, and all that; keep calm and carry on. I am not immersed because I am alone in my studio flat, shuttling between my desk and my bed, forcing myself through sit-ups on the carpet. I have exactly one window onto the world, and it looks directly onto a garden to which I have no access. The metaphors write themselves, and yet, sitting down to express them, I'm bereft.

I am trying to forgive myself for being unmoored to such an extent. To a point, the pace of the world has slowed to a degree where this is feasible. But I have it on good authority (from the people who pay my wages) that my work still needs to get done. Ultimately, whatever 'new normal' we've reached has one thing in common with the way we lived before: it's okay to not be okay, until such time as it interferes with someone else's bottom line. I am acutely conscious of how inconvenient I am as I struggle to do what needs to be done—professionally first, and then domestically, and (finally, as always) creatively.

Do I think the world will change? I feel just as precarious, just as thinly-stretched as I did before the virus went worldwide. If anything, the national mood here in England has become *more* jingoistic and hateful, not less. I don't have a great deal of faith.

But maybe I'm just too deep in the paint. I've watched my friends organise protests, build networks of mutual aid, create art that speaks to the possibilities they believe in. My small-c conservative parents have started to question the authority of the police. Immersion in one's own solitude and exhaustion is still immersion; I can't discount the possibility that the stagnation I feel is less than half of the story.

I want to believe it's a story I will write one day. I want to believe that I'll learn to see it clearly enough to tell it as it deserves to be told. I may not have confidence that the world at large will discover a better, braver way to be, in the grip of the kind of collective trauma that will shape us all in time — but I do believe that we will survive, and that when we tell the stories of how we survived, there will be a point. Call it cautious optimism. It's about the best I can do.

—June 26, 2020

Waverly SM is a speculative fiction writer preoccupied with apocalypses, impossible choices, and the ambient trauma of living in the world. They're a 2019 Lambda Literary Fellow and have been mentored, as part of a cohort of emerging LGBTQ+ voices, by Benjamin Alire Saenz. Waverly studied English at Newnham College, Cambridge; since then, their work has appeared in Argot Magazine, and will appear in *Stim: An Autism Anthology* (Unbound, forthcoming). They can currently be found trying to approximate the anchorite lifestyle in Oxford.

In the Flowery Countryside

Kelly Madden

Where shall we put the bodies, sir,
fifty thousand more today
and that is just at dawn
the cemetery's gates are chained,
undertaker's curtains drawn

curtains drawn good man? this will just not do
dig another trench, deep and wide;
but do not upset the people,
dig it out of sight

dig it out of sight dear sir?
the woods beyond the city are full,
there are few spaces now to hide
perhaps we should head further out,
in the flowery countryside?

in the flowery countryside? yes, good man, that might do
there is no time to spare
and do try to be good,
place them down with gentle care

place them down with gentle care, of course I want to sir,
but backhoe bucket does not allow
for gentleness in placing down;
perhaps some farmers will lend a hand

farmers might lend a hand good man?
indeed, this could save time,
now be sure to bury them deep enough
in the flowery countryside

in the flowery countryside is where I've been, sir,
and farmer's time was loaned

we did run out of markers, but
we marked the places with stones

marked the places with stones good man,
that was very kind
sadly now, you must stay
away from the flowery countryside

the farmers cry, no more! no more!
and leaders claim this problem is not theirs
perhaps the only thing to do now, good man
is load the trucks and head towards the capital city's front stairs

—July 4, 2020

Kelly Madden writes poetry and fiction. Her work has appeared in anthologies *Reckoning 2*, *Tending the Fire* (LCP chapbook), *Poetry Pause*, *Island Writer's Magazine* and elsewhere. She lives in the Comox Valley, BC.

Times and Seasons and Vanity upon Vanity

Tim Fab-Eme

I didn't know I could stop and trace the roads
of my palm the way my baby does, and tell
myself that moving fast isn't everything, that other folks had
walked this path, that Earth isn't mine alone, that am
not as great as I assumed, that it doesn't pay
to eat with both hands like crabs, that I'm vulnerable.

I didn't know I could live without sports and pop
myths, the lure of sex and the wild, the fantasy
of Hollywood and the charm of yachts. I didn't know.
Please, tell me again: why do you harm your neighbor
for the glory you met and will leave behind tomorrow?

I'm home now—the pandemic struck too fast for me
to shield myself as I always do when others mourn
the loss of the things they love. I'm quarantined from
all the things I bleached the ozone with my chimneys.

Reckon, there's a time for everything: a time for pollution
and a time we're chained from messing as we pleased,
a time to worship wealth and a time to croak

health is greater, a time for folly and a time
for duty, a time to crave the grandeur of greed

and a time to love everyone and everything as yourself.

—July 5, 2020

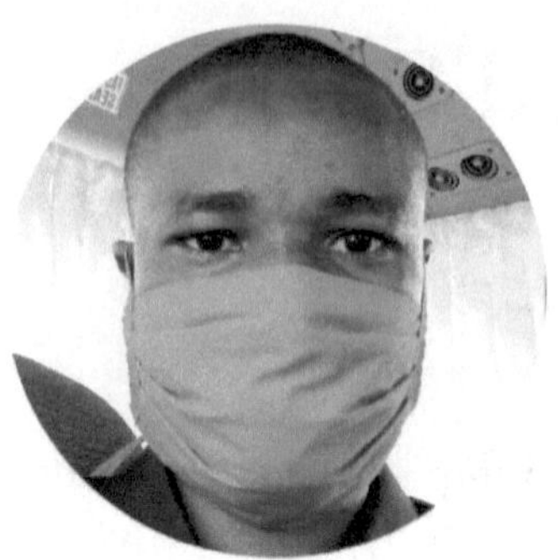

Tim Fab-Eme enjoys playing with poetic forms and the themes of identity, exploitation and the environment; he loves gardening and sometimes thinks himself a farmer. Tim hopes to revisit his long-abandoned prose manuscripts and treat them the way he treats his poetry manuscripts. He lives in Rivers; his work is published in *The Malahat Review*, *New Welsh Review*, *Magma*; *apt*, *The Fiddlehead* and *FIYAH*, etc. Tim studied engineering at the Niger Delta University, and is presently pursuing a BA in English Studies at the University of Port Harcourt.

Each day the world grows smaller & larger

Holly J. Hughes

as we retreat to our homes (those lucky to have them),
stock up on what we think we'll need—toilet paper,
hand sanitizer, flour, beans—begin to understand
what it means to hunker down. In public, try out
social distancing: smile, nod, nervous, wonder
is this six feet? when what we want is to embrace
every service person we meet: the efficient,
masked bagger at QFC, the weary pharmacist,
the stoic neighbor hobbling up the street.
The world now in our living room
and we watch in disbelief as bodies stack up
on nightly news, as doctors in Italy must choose
whose life to save. Meanwhile our phones beep
the rising Covid-19 count for our county,
new guidelines for gathering, from 250 to 50
to 10 in a week. Then tonight, on the news,
watch those exiled on ancient iron balconies,
the last common space, join their voices, reach across
what little divides—to fill the death-drenched air
with song: rock, arias, and last, their national anthem.
And from our living room, an ocean and a continent
away, we hear a voice, our own stubborn belief
in the human species, despite all the ways
we've bungled it, rise above the fear,
the uncertainty, the despair—join in.

—March 18, 2020

Holly J. Hughes is the author of *Hold Fast*, *Sailing by Ravens*, coauthor of *The Pen and The Bell: Mindful Writing in a Busy World*, and editor of the award-winning anthology, *Beyond Forgetting: Poetry and Prose about Alzheimer's Disease*. Her fine art chapbook *Passings* received an American Book Award from the Before Columbus Foundation in 2017. Her poems and essays have been nominated for Pushcart prizes and have appeared in a number of journals and anthologies, including *Poetry of Presence* and *Dancing with Joy*. She's a graduate of Pacific Lutheran University's low-residency MFA program, where she served on the staff for 13 years. She also spent over thirty summers working on the water in Alaska commercial fishing for salmon, skippering a 65-foot schooner and working as a naturalist on ships. She currently leads writing and mindfulness workshops in Alaska and the northwest and consults as a writing coach.

Love in the Time of Covid-19

James Treat

Dear editor,

I am submitting the personal ad below as a letter to the editor in order to save money for any possible coronavirus-related financial hardship I may encounter. Thank you in advance for waiving, in the spirit of the times, the normal fee for classifieds.

CNM seeks CNW

Coronavirus-negative man seeks coronavirus-negative woman for social distancing, lockdown, self-isolation, quarantine, hospitalization, possible long-term relationship. Let's avoid each other from the start! Especially interested in meeting compulsive handwashers and/or professional epidemiologists. Please, no asymptomatic super-spreaders. Attractive elbows a definite plus, though physical intimacy will be very limited for an unspecified period, subject to the dictates of government officials. Interested parties should transmit their astrological and vital signs to the CDC and await further instruction.

(s)James Treat
Silver City

—Originally appeared in the *Silver City Daily Press*, March 17, 2020

After an academic vocation teaching at several public research universities, James Treat is now an autonomous scholar, freelance creative, indigenous advocate, and nonviolent outdoorsman living in southwest New Mexico, within walking distance of the Continental Divide. His research focuses on **American Indian ways of knowing**, especially in the wake of imperial modernity. On a more theoretical level, he is interested in the **human ecology of indigenous societies** as a critique of industrial civilization. He writes literary nonfiction in various genres—reflexive scholarship, narrative history, topical essays, and found poetry. Much of his recent work has focused on the **Muscogee (Creek) Nation**, beginning with a monthly column on tribal traditions published in the *Muscogee Nation News*, reprinted by a dozen other periodicals, and archived at Mvskoke Country. He is currently writing a quarterly column for *POME Magazine*, another MCN publication, and working on related projects for their tribal enterprises. He is also completing a book manuscript titled *A Sort of Strange Land: Poems Found in Indian Territory*; previous versions of some of these pieces have been published in various literary and scholarly journals including *Reckoning 1*.

It's a Dark Time and I Try to Be a Light

Brian Francis Slattery

I've been interviewing artists of various kinds in New Haven since March about their response to the pandemic, and I've been telling people throughout that my job as a journalist has often been a real help, because I'm telling the stories of people who are adapting, people who are still working on things, who are sort of doing OK. I've also noticed that it seems sometimes like they're talking to each other, like they seem to be on the same page. What's below is constructed from quotes from 22 different people.

This virus is a horrifying gift—a life-and-death gift—for us to examine our priorities for how we want to be in this world. The system was set up for us to work too much and forget as much as possible. This has made us aware, if we didn't already know, of how on a wire our lives were.

It's not necessary for us to be stressed for the sake of productivity. If everyone just had $1,000 a month coming in from a value-added tax, people might be able to stay indoors and not have to risk their lives to get groceries. How robust a system can capitalism be if it needs to be bailed out by socialism every 10 years? If we didn't spend $90 billion on a bomb the size of Rhode Island, we could have a test kit in everybody's mailbox.

We are not going to go back as a society to the way it was before. People won't want to go back. We have to find out how to have the space to access that part of our brains and hearts, to take care of ourselves so we can take care of others. We got to lock arms and get through it together. What better way to uplift people's spirits than to do what we love to do? It's a dark time and I try to be a light.

I find a lot of solace in history as time goes on, because you see the patterns. This has happened, and people had to figure it out, and yet we're still here. Things continued. This is all just sort of a trial run—working out the kinks for what you have to do with climate change—anyway.

The danger isn't running out of stories; it's not telling them. I didn't have the time before to finish records, but now I do. Creatives always say that: We need more time. Now we have the time. We are understanding what a moment in time is. We can sit on a bench and think: light and leaves do that? Bathrooms are the cleanest they've ever been. They could be this clean all the time. People have a lot of time to work on stuff. Maybe we'll all learn how to farm and cook.

I'm not afraid of dying, We're all going to leave here; it's just how we go. I truly have a deep, deep trust that there is a lot going on that we don't understand, or can't wrap our heads around. I think my whole childhood and young adult life got me to this point. We have one life on this earth. I'm in my 50s. I want to eat every good thing in every day. I have all this wood laying around—a lot of random, found objects. I have a bag of paints and glues. I got some papier-mache. So I'll come up with something.

The future: We live there, it's weird. Hey—what are you going to do? Part of being an artist is getting in touch with your humanity. It's being vulnerable. We're all facing an existential threat. Connecting with people—it's why people keep showing up when it's so imperfect. This is the thing that reminds us of what it means to be human. That's what we want to capture when we get the chance, on the other side, when we're face to face. Even if we're six feet apart.

What do we see through the window? There was a nice day, and people were out and walking their dogs as if they had never been outside before. It is remarkable how good people are being to each other. Go outside and the spring is happening. The swamp maple is covered with little red furry blossoms. The iris is poking out from the ground. The daffodils are blooming like mad. Those are things that happen every year. This is not about the chaos. This is just Earth doing its thing. Every year it comes to life.

Don't give up. Work on you. Do some self-reflection, because once this thing lifts, we got to hit the ground running. We got work to do. There are forces in the unseen that can help us if we're open to them. There are ways of working that allow for repair to happen. Now more than ever, we have to reach out, figuring out ways of supporting each other. We have to reach out to something bigger than us. It's the new growth after a forest fire. Make new things. We're going into a new world. We need new songs.

—July 8, 2020

Brian Francis Slattery is a journalist and musician in New Haven, CT. He's the author of four published novels; for five years he was on the writing team for *Bookburners* (Serial Box), and his most recent fiction appears in *The New Decameron.*

Retreat, April 2, 2020

Adelia MacWilliam

After Tim Lilburn's poem, "Retreat."

When I was in Desolation Sound, during the pandemic, holed up in that bay,
its mornings and green tides and ravens, reading Tim Lilburn, it was so cold
in the mornings I'd put on five layers, feed the woodstove
until the kettle started to tick.
I'd stack firewood in the afternoons, the alder bark with its islands
of sepia and grey overlaid on cream, like an antique map
but studded with woodpecker holes
like tiny machine gun bullet holes,
as though attempting to obliterate the memories
of the world we'd just left behind.
Then I'd go rowing out into the Sound
toward the Unwin Mountains, rows of blue peaks receding into mist.
Also, I was tucking into Calvino's Six Memos for the Next Millennium,
literary values for future generations, his parliament on light
and the imagination. There was no hockey,
the NHL having cancelled the season, indeed, all seasons cancelled
except for nature's, getting a reprieve with this new quiet,
fish now visible in Venice's canals, the gondolas neatly stacked
across from the Basilica di San Marco.

Early morning rain fat with snow, unusual for April.
I didn't know exactly what I was lonely for.
Inchoate, this rite of passage into the world's ruin.

Adelia MacWilliam recently completed her MFA in poetry at the University of Victoria. She wrote about a piece of land that her family had "occupied" since 1905 and learned that if you cast the mythic imagination across a piece of land that has always been part of your life, everything will out. She is co-founder of Cascadia Poetics Lab, www.cascadiapoeticslab.ca, which produces the monthly Red Tree reading series. She divides her time between Vancouver Island and Desolation Sound. An emerging poet, her most recently published poem can be found in the anthology *Sweet Water: Poems for the Watersheds*, ed. Yvonne Blomer, Caitlin Press, 2020.

Escaping in a little boy's play.

Ernest Ifeanyi Nweke

It's been some cold four months. Even though our heaviest rainfalls happen between March and July, and are always chaperoned by intense heat, these months have been cold ones. Somehow, the months had the biting loneliness and endlessness one only gets on cold nights. Living, for those of us that haven't died, has been like lying in a large bed in December with no coverings, in a room with large open windows. Alone. Wondering when morning will come, if morning will come.

What I have done the most in these days and months has been watch. I watched because in watching you're persons removed, you're apart from the pains and the confusion. I watched my four year old nephew who got so little time to watch cartoons when we all soaked our eyes in Al jazeera resort to staging plays with his pairs of slippers, and cups, and sticks. I watched as people who once had full lives, who went to the gym and planned diets they knew they'd not stick to and holidays they could never afford became reduced to numbers and cases. When I went out to buy vegetables from the small market at a junction not so far from my house, I watched faces that knew so little of what was happening in the world outside their front doors and stalls forced to close up shop early or close altogether and go hungry without explanations or provisions.... Watching was a lot of comfort but at the same time a lot of pain.

While counting the cold days from March to July, and watching, I wrote poetry. I didn't write poetry because I wanted to bide time as my cousin did when he opened a Tiktok account to follow trends of short videos. I wrote poems because that was the only way I could stay sane. I wrote poems because I needed to stop talking to myself and I couldn't stop talking to myself knowing that people who once had full lives, beautiful lives, sad lives, all kinds of lives were now nothing but numbers and cases.

The poems, all twenty of them, were imagined lives and significant others of the cases and numbers. Some recovered and went home others died and others faced agony within white walls and under bright lights and the stench of disinfectants, not knowing if they will live to go home or not. I hoped that these imaginary lives would add some warmth to the coldness of numbers.

When I wasn't watching the news, wishing I could give those cold words and numbers the broadcasters called out a hug, I was watching my nephew, all William in his Globe, casting Romeo and Juliet, and having them live happily ever after. Thinking back now, I marvel at the escapism his plays offered him and I; creativity rescued me from the chill of numbers.

—July 30, 2020

Ernest Ifeanyi Nweke would have loved to describe himself as "he of whom nothing must be written about" just so he would escape writing a bio, but that didn't seem appropriate. He's a sucker for vintage movies. When he's not seeking out art of different forms to devour, he is writing the best stories the world will ever see in his head.

COVID Summer: After, Now

Marissa Lingen

There will be rooms of people
You've never seen before.
And won't again, strangers,
Brazenly loving music,
Eating dumplings, browsing scarves.
There will be breaths let out,
Unchecked; there will be strange air,
Strange beds, cafe tables
That wobble as you write.
There will be spontaneous outings.
You will linger in the ice cream shop,
Not hurry out to lick your cone
In the street; you will rush
Between drinks and a show,
Take a cab, hug a friend. Now
There are calculations, comparisons,
Care. Familiar walls and making do,
And it does. But only for now.

—July 31, 2020

COVID Summer: Against Dystopia

Marissa Lingen

They ask her if this is the end,
Armageddon, Ragnarok—is Jesus
Going to come sort this. Can it get
Worse. Winston Smith knew
Dystopia is not drama but grind,
The constant scrape of fear.
We've tried dramatic speeches
(Appalling, sublime); it's time
To get on with the slow business
Of building, growing from seed,
Rejecting the martyr for the maker.

—July 31, 2020

Marissa Lingen is a freelance writer living in the suburbs of Minneapolis with her family. Mostly she writes speculative fiction. She has a large collection of foliage-themed jewelry.

Writing in the Time of Coronavirus 2

Giselle Leeb

One thing that's been blooming in this coronavirus crisis is dreams. Near the beginning of lockdown, a friend told me hers: the landscape outside her house was destroyed. But it was replaced by a green cactus with kangaroo-bear hybrids lolloping round it. It seemed to symbolise devastation and enforced change, but something new and tougher was growing from it.

My latest story involves a prison, and a tremendous sense of longing for and guilt about what we've lost through our destruction of the environment. Oddly, we'd succeeded in displacing ourselves. As I've had more time to listen to the birds singing above the traffic, and to observe a chopped-down tree continuously sending out new shoots in the back garden, I've been cheered by nature's astonishing tenacity, and saddened at how, if we don't get our arses into gear, we won't be a part of it. Already, we barely belong.

What has also crept into my writing is paying more attention to all of the senses, but especially touch. Currently single, not touching people feels like a dismemberment of something crucial: connection through the body. I've written quite a few stories about apes and this strange absence makes me think about how they touch each other continuously, and how the warmth of another body bypasses the mind and hooks into the sense of belonging necessary to all human beings.

I've been wracking my brains about how this sense of belonging can help overcome the enormity of the climate crisis facing us. People's actions during the covid crisis are a giant crucible, reflecting how we've acted in the past and showing how we could do things differently in the future.

There are no goals for me in writing fiction, only open-endedness: feeling my way, seeing what comes up, and following it. It's the opposite of the control and dehumanisation inherent in the late-capitalist view of what a human should be like.

Writing constantly surprises me with the answers I find,

without trying to, answers that seem to come from the sum of my experience with other human beings, which is why I think of writing as a communal act.

So, who knows how writing fiction can help change the world. Some submission calls ask you to imagine a positive future. That has its place. But writing about the sadness of the world could just as easily change something. The reader's absorption of the writing is as mysterious as the process of creation. How to put a value on such a subtle, but real, thing? Which is why it's so hard to fund the arts in our hyper-capitalist society.

But don't you always remember that thing you read years ago, that you've never forgotten, that in fact changed your life?

Whatever happens, I know I'm going to keep on with this odd activity called writing, that is all about exploring and possibilities, without pressure. The crisis has affirmed this for me.

—August 26, 2020

Giselle Leeb grew up in South Africa and lives in Nottingham. Her short stories have appeared in over thirty publications including *Best British Short Stories 2017* (Salt), *Lady Churchill's Rosebud Wristlet*, *Black Static*, *Mslexia*, *Litro*, and other places. She is a Word Factory Apprentice Award winner and an assistant editor at *Reckoning Journal*. Her story, Scaffolding, is forthcoming in *Mainstream*, an anthology of stories from the edges, by Inkandescent Press.
http://giselleleeb.com
Twitter: @gisellekleeb

In Isolation

Andrew Kozma

In isolation, I thought maybe nature was the answer. No other humans, just the organic Earth and everything else that lived on it. If we were the lice, then all those other plants and animals were what? The too-tiny-to-see worms inhabiting our eyelashes? All the microorganisms living on our bodies, unnoticed until something goes wrong and the benign skin bacteria begins to rot the blood?

The metaphor got away from me. It's useless anyway. Language is for communicating with other humans. The world doesn't care what we call it.

And so I took long walks at midnight. Sometimes I heard frogs. Sometimes crickets. Sometimes birds whose bodies were fooled by the glow of the city that never died. Sometimes someone else walking the sidewalks, face also masked. Everything went quiet when I passed, ghosting like a dream I couldn't shake.

In my fourplex, the sounds of my housemates were distant. Practicing drums. Loud and laugh-salted phone conversations. The thud and groans of home exercise or masturbation. There was no passing each other in the front entry. No hellos. The cars drove themselves out in the morning and parked themselves at night. Packages delivered on the front steps walked their way inside.

I was lucky to have this luxury of isolation. I had savings. A job I could do online. When I went to the grocery store, I eyed everyone with suspicion, and they suspected me right back. This would bring us closer, I remember an op-ed claiming. Distance makes the heart grow fonder. People are more compassionate with the suffering they can't see.

A shaky claim, but I'd bought into it.

But in the grocery store and the post office where other people were unavoidable, all I saw were the eyes and the upper part of the face, eyebrows angled down, foreheads wrinkled in annoyance and fear. Do you know the way an ear moves when a person frowns so deeply their face collapses in on itself? Or how the throat visibly tightens if you're straining to hold back a scream?

I practiced in the mirror, eliminating all the telltale signs visible around the mask. It is so much safer to be a blank slate, reflecting nothing. With all the masks, how can we know who to hold accountable? By the time the mask is off, it's too late.

Months passed. The world evolved. Civilization adjusted. Every online meeting I attended, I blanked my camera. My cat became a great conversationalist. Television windowed a world that was and would never be again.

Oh, not even that is the truth, I can tell you now. There was an alternate universe in old photographs, one which never even existed. Or if it existed, it was always an illusion with as much solidity as a soap bubble. The illusion popped and our eyes are stinging and we can choose to keep our eyes closed or wash them out and look around us with a new, pained vision.

I say we because it's easier than saying I.

Here's the truth.

We are each in a tiny spaceship, a bubble just large enough for us and the supplies to survive. An attic efficiency in space. Bed. Kitchen. Exercise machine. Entertainment box. Each ship can survive indefinitely, which is good, because each of us is traveling through space for an indefinite time. Like dandelion seeds, we have been blown from Earth and shot out into the vastness of the empty black.

Food and water are effectively infinite. Air, too. Everything is recycled. Nano-machines ever carefully clear the air of the dust made by our flaking skin and shed hair. Something something relativism makes it so we age virtually not at all. And communication between us is equally magical and instantaneous. There are explanations for why it all works, but the science doesn't matter. Whether we understand how and why we are here, here is where we are. In an enclosed space, each of us alone.

Hello? Can you hear me? If you can hear me, press the red flashing button.

One day we'll travel beyond the Sun's encompassing light and it'll shrink to be just another star. Already, all the planets are invisible except by computer projection. I know your voice is out there. So just press the button to open the link.

All we have is each other.

—September 9, 2020

Andrew Kozma's fiction has been published in *Escape Pod*, *Mythic*, *Daily Science Fiction*, and *Analog*. His book of poems, *City of Regret* (Zone 3 Press, 2007), won the Zone 3 First Book Award.

Portrait by Wolf William Say.

Grieving Season

Rachel Watts

I take my father's ghost and a crochet bird nest with me. The air is clean and clear, my body is empty, and no-one mentions the war. It is January. The nest is a half-built tiny home for a tiny injured thing. The left-over yarn I'm using is messy as life, cobbled together. An emergency measure.

We already know which cities will go dry. Which will be flooded.
I tuck the nest, with hook and yarn, into a (reused) paper bag.
And somewhere there is an animal. The last of its kind.

In March, we are sent to our homes, while we still have them.

We've already forgotten islands. We've already forgotten fire.

I fold my father's ghost and slip it between my ribs. I wear my grandmother's thin Irish skin as a mask and learn how to breathe. Nothing is wasted. My liver came down from my Grandfather.

We are sent to our homes.

On the TV the rich men take turns.

And somewhere is an animal. The last of its kind.

I have forgotten the unfinished birds' nest by August, until I find it on a side table. It is made of left-over strings of yarn in every colour and it is the ugliest thing I've ever created. I remember when I sat watching the world on fire. All I could do was twist and hook with great seriousness.

On the TV the men don't mention tiny birds and their vaporised homes.

The people are dying (heart disease, cancer).

The people are dying (suicide, hunger, mosquito).

The people are dying (virus unknown).

"People really die and no longer one by one," Sigmund Freud said (Freud, via Victoriano, 2003 212).

On the TV the men come and go but there's never time to grieve.

Fire season is nearly here again.

And somewhere there is an animal, the last of its kind.

I am 11 years old, sitting under a tree next to the river. A migraine peels apart my brain. My grandma's cool hand on my face.

"Just let the pain in, don't resist," she says. "Relax. The pain comes from resisting."

I relax my mind. The seagulls wheel.

The tree holds us in its shade.

Here's the pain I let in: I have stopped thinking about the baby bird. (I think of it as a baby but it could just be very, very small). I'm slow at crochet and not very good with babies either, having never had one wanted one, having never seen the need.

But now the world is full of endings and somewhere an animal is the last of its kind.

My Grandma's cool hand on my skin.

The world is full of endings and I am the daughter of a daughter.

I will never have a daughter.

And somewhere, an animal is the last of its kind.

There are no ultimatums with ghosts.

My dad is a ghost who, when living, would enter the country in secret, so he could surprise us after school. Thirty years before every kid in the country saw the animal corpses. Thirty years before we started baking bread with fervour, stuck at home, safe at home, neither, never. He leans in, all paper, and reminds me that it was him. That he told them where to dig for the oil and the gas.

Here, on Noongar country, I was born, he was born, his dad was born, and before that, the boat, the English towns, the Irish fields. The sky is clear, there is no emergency for white folks, until there is.

And somewhere there's an animal. The last of its kind.

Dropping its bones for the future (what future?) to name.

I tuck his ghost back between my ribs, I take him with me to the protest march. But my voice is stuck, there are feathers and guilt in my throat.

On the TV, the rich men come and go.

Fire season is nearly here again.

"People really die, and no longer one by one," Dr Freud said. "It is no longer an accident." (Freud, via Victoriano, 2003 212).

And somewhere there is an animal, the last of its kind.

The Noongar calendar has six seasons, because December is different to February, but they all burn just the same these days.

The ghost of my dad folds up small. A beginning, an ending, an origami weight of never growing old.

It's eleven seconds to midnight. The rich men wear suits and wave showbusiness hands.

Now is not the time.

Now is not time.

Now is not.

I thought there'd be more shouting, at the end.

And somewhere, there is an animal.

The last of its kind.

—January - September, 2020

Works cited

Victoriano, Filipe, Aaron Walker and Carl Good *Fiction, Death and Testimony: Toward a Politics of the Limits of Thought*, Discourse 25, (2003): 211-230. Sourced at http://www.jstor.org/stable/41389671.

Rachel Watts is a writer of literary and speculative fiction and creative non-fiction. Her work has been published by *Westerly Magazine*, *Island*, *Kill Your Darlings*, *The Big Issue* and more. She works as a tutor and lives on the unceded lands of the Whadjuk people of the Noongar nation. www.wattswrites.com @watts_writes

Kondottiyans

Fabiyas M V

The repatriation flight skids off the tabletop runaway,
thundering in the tailwind.
Homing dreams crash through the optical illusion.

Breaking the pandemic shackles,
they gallop toward the gruesome gorge.
Downpour and darkness cannot immure their vigor.
They are incandescent with compassion,
forget their masks.
Excruciating voices.
They hasten to hospitals,
carrying the passengers in PPE kits,
who are either dead or dying.
Their WhatsApp messages multiply agile hands.
They wait before the blood banks.
The forlorn kids are glued to their hearts with the love-epoxy.

They return home to quarantine themselves
at dawn.
Humans aren't extinct among men.

—September 20, 2020

Fabiyas M V is a writer from Orumanayur village in Kerala, India. He is the author of *Monsoon Turbulence* (Poetry Nook, US) *Shelter within the Peanut Shells* (Red Cherry Books, India), *Kanoli Kaleidoscope* (PunksWritePoemsPress,US), *Eternal Fragments* (erbacce press, UK), *Stringless Lives* (Budding Light Press, Australia), *Moonlight And Solitude* (Raspberry Books, India). His fiction and poetry have appeared in several anthologies, magazines and journals. Western Australian University, British Council, University of Hawaii, Rosemont College, Douglas College, Forward Poetry, Off the Coast, Silver Blade, Pear Tree Press, Poetry Nook, Zoetic Press, Typehouse, Structo, Encircle Publications, Pendle War Poetry and Creative Writing Ink are some of his publishers. He has won many international accolades including Merseyside at War Poetry Award from Liverpool University; Lest We Forget Poetry Prize from Auckland War Memorial Museum; and Animal Poetry Prize 2012 from RSPCA (Royal Society for Prevention of Cruelties against Animals, UK). He was the finalist for Global Poetry Prize 2015 by the United Poets Laureate International (UPLI) in Vienna. His poems have been broadcast on All India Radio. Poetry Nook, US, has nominated him for the 2019 Pushcart Prize. He has been working as a teacher in English at Gov. Higher Secondary School, Maranchery in Kerala.

Green Papayas on a Sunday Evening

Shikhandin

TIDINGS

A harried wind has come

bearing in his arms
ill tidings.

Ratt-a-tatting timidly
on my door,
head hanging low,
hat in hand, my rain-drenched wind
pleads to be let in.

But I do not want him
in. I quickly shut my windows, and
stuff all the nooks and crannies.
I even cotton up my ears,
because I know.

Oh! I know. Don't I know what my wind
has come to say?

He's come to say the world is in utter disarray.
And, that I am weak and powerless. That I
can do nothing! Dear God! I can do nothing
but watch the horror unfold.

Perhaps I was being prescient when I wrote this poem before the world changed. I don't know. All I know is that there is an odd stillness in my heart now. And the face of that woman selling green papayas is haunting me.

That Sunday evening seems like a distant dream today. We left the city of Hyderabad a few Sundays ago, and are still settling down in our own home, even as I write this piece. The shadow of the virus dims our sun. The numbers have climbed up so high, India now practically leads the global pandemic. Covid 19 has swept out from the cities into the hinterlands, where basic healthcare is negligent, forget Covid care. The virus has even entered our tiny community of seventy-two homes. An eerie silence wheels around the children's play area. And that mainstay of Indian homes, the daily help, is missing. The sharp edges of people have softened since the early days of Covid. Neighbours are no longer discriminatory towards those in quarantine. Our face masks have created a fraternity which wasn't there before. There is little difference between our lives in Hyderabad and Chennai. Except that here, in lieu of a large balcony, I have a terrace I can run up to, and stand beneath a vast rolling sky. It provides a respite from the walls. In Hyderabad, we needed to rush out of our homes just to get some fresh air.

That Sunday was no different. My husband and I drove towards Hyderabad's older parts, where people live cheek by jowl, and the shops are open-to-the-sky carts and wooden platforms. Hyderabad's historical monuments, the Golkonda fort, Kutab Shahi tombs and further down, the Charminar and Falak Nama Palace, are located there. I wanted to see them as we drove past. So, we went, armed with face masks, hand sanitisers, a large bottle of water, and a shopping bag, in case we found something to buy!

We cruised around, safe inside our mobile egg (that is what Arvind Adiga called cars in his Booker award winning book 'The White Tiger'). The evening sky had turned into a violet velvet cape, pinned up by the brightest Jupiter of the year. The narrow roads were chock-a-block with people. It was in fact a scene straight out of a village fair, a mela. There were men selling shocking pink cotton candy on sticks, balloons, cheap plastic toys, spicy crispy fried snacks in newspaper cones, corn on the cobs roasting on charcoal stoves on trolleys. People sat with their wares laid out on plastic sheets on the dirt tracks beside the narrow road. Second-hand clothes, rubber footwear, folding umbrellas, fruits and vegetables.

Nobody seemed to care about safety. Most of them did not have masks on. They were obviously not practising social distancing, but were laughing, talking, backslapping and hugging each other with abandon. Some women and children crowded around a handpump, gossiping or playing as they waited their turn to draw water. The scene was a far cry from the other India of glass and concrete towers, air-conditioned homes and malls, and all the necessities and luxuries available in all developed countries. A world we too are privy to.

If anything, Covid 19 has outlined the thousand-headed social divide in India with thick black indelible lines. The have-nots out-number the haves by far despite the strides India has made in the past decade. Online classes are a privilege the majority of Indian school children cannot afford. What the world knows about India is always a few notches off the mark, whether it is the good, the bad or the ugly. This subject is so complex and convoluted that it cannot be explained away in a few lines or even chapters! But if I were to draw a quick sketch, I'd say that those who are subjugated and deprived in India face it from so many angles that they have no fear left. They leave it all to fate. In their world, they have only each other. This was the spirit I observed all around me from behind my rolled-up car window, as we negotiated our way past the human throngs, stray goats and cows, and unruly traffic. And, we also saw the papayas!

"Want to pick up a few?" said my husband in all seriousness.

The woman selling the fruit understood from long experience that she had a potential customer. Her body shifted, almost imperceptibly. I knew if I gestured, she would bring a few over for me to choose.

Raw-green papayas are nutritious and delicious. Their most famous avatar may be the Thai salad, but their buttery texture when boiled and mashed makes them a great substitute for mashed potatoes with roast pork or beef. A pat of butter, salt and pepper is all you need. Bengalis, like us, love them grated and steamed with whole aromatic spices like bay leaves, green cardamoms, cloves and cinnamon, and topped with shredded coconut and clarified butter. My mouth watered. It had been a while since we had eaten them. Even from a distance, and in the fading light, I could tell how fresh these were. Glossy jade green, with their cut stems still oozing the milky sap.

"You think it's worth the risk?" I said, even as my fingers itched to touch them. "I mean, nobody's following any safety rules here."

My husband swerved just then, taking most of the car out of the road and onto the dirt track. A gleaming Range Rover Autobiography muscled its way forward. A man in his late thirties or early forties was at the wheel. He barely noticed our much smaller vehicle. Irritated, I looked away. At that instant the eyes of the woman with the perfect green papayas met mine. She smiled with compassion at this privileged woman, fearful of the poor and angry at the uber rich. Her eyes seemed to fling questions at me: Would I recoil if my hands involuntarily touched hers? Would I rush home to disinfect myself?

We drove back home without the coveted papayas. Some weeks later we relocated. The young men from the packers and movers kept their masks on in our presence. But took them off blithely during their lunch break. To them we were delicate creatures, not of robust flesh and blood like themselves. Yet we are all brethren under the Indian sky. And, if the little poem I wrote was prescient, my sentiments were wrong. One can always do something, no matter how insignificant. That small something may be a thought in the mind or a feeling, but it is still a shift towards change.

Gratitude for what we have. Frugal and mindful living. Respect for this world and all in it. And outrage at what we have knowingly and unknowingly done. These may sound like platitudes mouthed by a woman living a sheltered life, but to quote Benjamin Franklin, "Justice will not be served until those who are unaffected are as outraged as those who are."

Shikhandin is the pen name of an Indian writer. Her published books include "Impetuous Women" (Penguin-Random House India), "Immoderate Men" (Speaking Tiger), and "Vibhuti Cat" (Duckbill-Penguin-Random House India). Prior to that a novel and a short story collection were published. Shikhandin's honours include, runner up George Floyd Short Story Contest 2020 (UK), Pushcart nominee by Aeolian Harp (USA) 2019, Pushcart nominee by Cha: An Asian Literary Journal (Hong Kong) 2011, Winner 2017 Children First Contest curated by Duckbill in association with Parag an initiative of Tata Trust, First prize Brilliant Flash Fiction Contest 2019 (USA), Runner up Erbacce Poetry Prize (UK), Winner 35th Moon Prize (Writing in a Woman's Voice: USA), First Runner up The DNA-OoP Short Story Contest 2016 (India), Second Prize India Currents Katha Short Story Contest 2016 (USA), First prize Anam Cara Short Fiction Competition 2012 (Ireland), Long list Bridport Poetry Prize 2006 (UK), Finalist Aesthetica Poetry Contest 2010 (UK). Shikhandin's poetry and prose have been widely published in journals and anthologies worldwide.

Amazon Page: https://www.amazon.com/author/shikhandin
Facebook: https://www.facebook.com/AuthorShikhandin/
Instagram: https://www.instagram.com/writershikhandin/
Twitter: @Shikhandintweet

www.ingramcontent.com/pod-product-compliance
Lightning Source LLC
Chambersburg PA
CBHW021739190726
48288CB00009B/3116

9781955360029